EBCDIC	Extended Binary Coded Decimal Interchange Code	**IPSec**	IP Security
EIA	Electronics Industries Association	**IRTF**	Internet Research Task Force
ESP	Encapsulating Security Payload	**ISO**	International Organization of Standardization
ESS	extended service set	**ISOC**	Internet Society
FCC	Federal Communications Commission	**ISP**	Internet service provider
FCS	frame check sequence	**ITU-T**	International Telecommunications Union–Telecommunication Standardization Sector
FHSS	frequency hopping spread spectrum	**KDC**	key distribution center
FQDN	fully qualified domain name	**LAN**	local area network
FTAM	File Transfer, Access, and Management	**LCP**	Link Control Protocol
FTP	File Transfer Protocol	**LIS**	logical IP subnet
HDSL	high bit rate digital subscriber line	**LSA**	link state advertisement
HTML	Hypertext Markup Language	**MAA**	message access agent
HTTP	Hypertext Transfer Protocol	**MBONE**	multicast backbone
IAB	Internet Architecture Board	**MIB**	management information base
IANA	Internet Assigned Numbers Authority	**MILNET**	Military Network
ICANN	Internet Corporation for Assigned Names and Numbers	**MIME**	Multipurpose Internet Mail Extension
ICMP	Internet Control Message Protocol	**MOSPF**	Multicast Open Shortest Path First
IEEE	Institute of Electrical and Electronics Engineers	**MSS**	maximum segment size
IESG	Internet Engineering Steering Group	**MTA**	message transfer agent
IETF	Internet Engineering Task Force	**MTU**	maximum transfer unit
IGMP	Internet Group Management Protocol	**NAP**	Network Access Point
INTERNIC	Internet Network Information Center	**NAT**	network address translation
IP	Internetworking Protocol	**NCP**	Network Control Protocol
IPng	Internetworking Protocol, next generation	**NFS**	network file system
		NIC	Network Information Center
		NIC	network interface card
		NNI	network-to-network interface
		NSF	National Science Foundation